DUBSTEP'S ORIGINS WERE FOUND IN SOUTH LONDON IN THE EARLY 2000S, AROUND THE SAME TIME AS GRIME WAS STARTING TO CAUSE DAMAGE TO THE AIRWAVES, AND UK GARAGE HAD GONE FULLY DARKSIDE.

ARTISTS WERE FUSING TOGETHER SYNCOPATED DUB BASSLINES, SOUNDSYSTEM SAMPLES & A BLEND OF 2-STEP & HALFTIME BEATS. CROYDON'S BIG APPLE RECORDS & AMMUNITION'S FWD>> NIGHT PLAYED A MAJOR ROLE IN BRINGING THIS SOUND TO THE FOREFRONT OF UNDERGROUND DANCE MUSIC.

THIS BOOK HIGHLIGHTS SOME OF THE LABELS RATED 'THE BIGGEST & BADDEST' AS WELL AS SHOWING OFF THE NEW SCHOOL & THE GODFATHERS WHO PAVED THE WAY SO FAR & THOSE CRAFTING THE EMERGING FUTURE SOUNDS OF DUBSTEP!

Words
Chris Dexta &
Sam Rice (Yeti)

Editor
Colin Steven

Design
Banana Gun

Publishers
Southside Circulars
& Velocity Press

First edition
March 2023

southsidecirculars.com
velocitypress.uk

VP025

ISBN: 978-1-913231-42-2

THE ICON CATALOGUE
DUBSTEP
VOL. 1

01. 1985
02. 2ND DROP
03. ARTIKAL
04. BARE DUBS
05. BIG APPLE
06. BLACK ACRE
07. BOKA
08. CONTAGIOUS
09. DEEP HEADS
10. DEEP MEDI
11. DISFIGURED DUBZ
12. DUB POLICE
13. ENCRYPTED AUDIO
14. FAT KID ON FIRE
15. FIRMLY ROOTED
16. GHOST
17. HEMLOCK
18. HOTLINE
19. HYPERDUB
20. INNAMIND
21. JUAN FORTE
22. LION CHARGE
23. LIVITY SOUND
24. NOMINE SOUND
25. ON THE EDGE
26. RANKING RECORDS
27. SCRUB A DUB
28. SECTOR 7
29. SENTRY
30. SKULL DISCO
31. SMOKIN SESSIONS
32. SOUTHSIDE DUBSTERS
33. SUBALTERN
34. SUB:CLEF
35. SYSTEM
36. TEMPA
37. UPRISE AUDIO
38. WELL ROUNDED DUBS
39. WHITE PEACH
40. ZAM ZAM SOUNDS

1985

2015 - PRESENT

1985 was originally a D&B / Halfstep imprint, but since 2015 has dropped Dubstep consistently from some of the scene's freshest talent, such as Cesco, Drone, Monty and label owner Alix Perez himself.

THE ESSENTIALS

ALIX PEREZ 'LAST RITES'

TRAIL 'VELASQUEZ'

2ND DROP

2007 - 2016

Home to early works from Djrum & J:Kenzo. Certainly more leaning on the more melodic and stripped-back sound that was going down around the time. Other artists include Ramadanman, LV & Rusko.

THE ESSENTIALS

DJ RUM 'MOUNTAINS, PT.1'

J:KENZO 'CONQUEROR'

ARTIKAL

2012 - PRESENT

J:Kenzo's legendary Dubstep label; used as a home to house his own music and provide a platform for many rising names in the scene, such as CIMM, Mystic State, Sleeper & TMSV.

THE ESSENTIALS

MYSTIC STATE 'MAHDI'

THELEM 'HAUNTED HARMONICS'

BARE DUBS

2006 - 2008

Very short-lived imprint from Deapoh, but it released Dubstep heavyweights such as Kromestar, L-Wiz, Ramadanman & Tes La Rock

THE ESSENTIALS

KROMESTAR 'ZULU DANCE'

L WIZ 'PIRATES'

BIG APPLE RECORDS

2001 - 2007

The label responsible for the whole Dubstep genre! Run from the Croydon shop (where Hatcha cut his teeth) of the same name. Home to debut releases from Artwork, Benga, Digital Mystikz, Loefah & Skream

THE ESSENTIALS

ARTWORK 'RED'

DIGITAL MYSTIKZ 'PATHWAYS'

BLACK ACRE

2007 - PRESENT

Launched by Ian Merchant (label manager of Bristol's now defunct Chemical Records) - heavily supporting the city and paving the way for their own branch of Dubstep!

THE ESSENTIALS

COMMODO 'HOW WHAT TIME LP'

SULLY 'VAMP'

2005 - 2021

Truly pioneering label from the UK, whilst also making space for international talent too. Heat from MRK1, Distance & Emalkay - not to be missed!

THE ESSENTIALS

DJ DISTANCE 'REPLICANT'

16 BIT 'IN THE DEATH CAR'

CONTAGIOUS

2002 - 2010

Label dropping more of a darker sound of Dubstep, founded by Virus Syndicate producer Mark One (MRK1). Featured early works from big guns such as Chimpo, Jack Sparrow, Plastician & MRK1 himself.

THE ESSENTIALS

JACK SPARROW ‘I AND I’

MRK1 ‘KILL ZONE’

DEEP HEADS

2010 - PRESENT

Respected dubstep imprint from Zeb Samuels (Smokin Sessions / On The Edge Records), pushing a more ambient, jazz-infused style of Dubstep. Releases from Biome, Congi, Kromestar & Synkro.

THE ESSENTIALS

KROMESTAR 'BOOOKEY'

BIOME 'HAVANA'

DEEP MEDI

2006 - PRESENT

DEEP MEDI

Picking up where DMZ left off, Mala has been setting the pace and innovating nonstop since the label's debut in 2006. Fun fact - every release has a portrait of the artist drawn by Tunnidge.

THE ESSENTIALS

MARK PRITCHARD 'ELEPHANT DUB'
COMMODO 'STRAIGHT REPTILLIAN'

DISFIGURED DUBZ

2007 - 2012

DISFIGURED DUBZ

After Skream rose to the forefront of the Dubstep scene, it was only natural he'd start his own imprint, bringing through artists such as CluekiD, Kryptic Mindz, Phaelah, to name a few.

THE ESSENTIALS

SKREAM & CLUEKID 'SANDSNAKE'

DIGITAL MYSTIKZ 'SHAKE OUT YOUR DEMONS'

DUB POLICE

2005 - 2015

Putting out hit after hit from Dubstep royalty like Caspa, Emalkay, L Wiz & Rusko. They garnered a whole load of attention and held a long-standing monthly night at London's iconic fabric nightclub.

THE ESSENTIALS

THE OTHERS 'AFRICA'

CASPA 'COCKNEY VIOLIN'

ENCRYPTED AUDIO

2014 - PRESENT

Run between London and Austin, Texas by Content & Deafblind and has been releasing dubstep artillery consistently for nearly ten years, with heat from Argo, Rgyby, Chokez & Samba...

THE ESSENTIALS

SAMBA & CHOKEZ 'GHASTLY'

EVA808 'MARANE'

FAT KID ON FIRE

2011 - PRESENT

FatKidOnFire's Wil Benton has gone from blogging and sharing mixes to launching the label and DJing around the world. Still premiering the freshest 140bpm beats - he's done a lot for the scene already!

THE ESSENTIALS

TAIKO 'DON'T BE STOOPID FT. SKITTLES'

MALLEUS 'VODUN'

FIRMLY ROOTED

2019 - PRESENT

Bristol-based collective, soundsystem & record label focusing on the more roots / dubwise sound of Dubstep, with releases from Halcyonic, Breakfake, Junior Dread & RSD.

THE ESSENTIALS

HALCYONIC & JUNIOR DREAD 'CAN'T HIDE (RSD REMIX)'
PANIX & LIONPULSE 'RUDEBOY STANCE'

GHOST

2000 - 2002 / 2007 - PRESENT

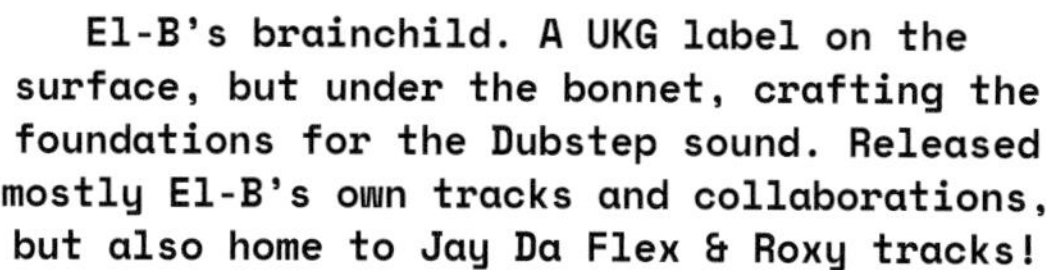

El-B's brainchild. A UKG label on the surface, but under the bonnet, crafting the foundations for the Dubstep sound. Released mostly El-B's own tracks and collaborations, but also home to Jay Da Flex & Roxy tracks!

THE ESSENTIALS

EL-B 'DANCEHALL EP'

GHOST 'WE AINT PLAYIN'

HEMLOCK

2008 - 2021

For the most part, Dubstep of the more melodic/electronic kind. Home to the debut release from James Blake and also music from Pangaea & Pearson Sound, Randomer and label boss, Berlin-based Untold.

THE ESSENTIALS

JAMES BLAKE 'AIR & LACK THEREOF'
UNTOLD 'I CAN'T STOP THIS FEELING (PANGAEA RMX)'

HOTLINE RECORDINGS

2012 - PRESENT

Established in Bristol in 2012, this is a label not to be pigeonholed. Ranging from Ishan Sounds' dubbed-out sound - to sneaky Grime bangers from Hi5 Ghost. Definitely one to check out!

THE ESSENTIALS

ISHAN SOUND 'DUB MINDSET (E3 DUB)'

KAHN & NEEK 'BACKCHAT'

HYPERDUB

2004 - PRESENT

With its origins rooted in the Dubstep world, Kode 9's label was responsible for releasing the elusive Burial and his many works. Also home to LV, Ikonika & Zomby and heavyweight tunes like Skeng.

THE ESSENTIALS

BURIAL 'SOUTH LONDON BOROUGHS'

THE BUG FT KILLA P & FLOWDAN 'SKENG'

INNAMIND

2011 - PRESENT

Well-respected stateside imprint brought to you by Kursk with releases from the likes of Quest, Gantz, Thelem, Karma, TMSV and Boofy. You can see where this is going - legendary status!

THE ESSENTIALS

QUEST 'VAMPIRES'

GANTZ 'ENSO / SIYAM'

JUAN FORTE

2019 - PRESENT

Started by a network of soundsytem fans, focusing on the authentic sounds of Dubstep and creating mad hype with their top-notch artwork and visual marketing campaigns. Deep wallets needed if you want 'em all!

THE ESSENTIALS

RAREMAN 'SHIBUYA NIGHTZ'

FEARLESS DREAD 'N4'

LION CHARGE

2013 - PRESENT

J:Kenzo's dubwise imprint, pushing the sound of some of the scene's more 'new school' troops such as Adam Prescot, Digid, DJ Madd, Kaiju & Sabab.

THE ESSENTIALS

KILLAWATT & IPMAN 'JIGSAW DUB'

KAIJU 'UNITY DUB'

LIVITY SOUND

2011 - PRESENT

While not strictly a Dubstep label, Peverelist and his Livity Sound label are more on the Bass/Experimental side of the scene, fusing Techno, Dubstep beats and basslines.

THE ESSENTIALS

PEV & KOWTON 'BENEATH RADAR'

PEV & KOWTON 'VAPOURS'

NOMINE SOUND

2016 - PRESENT

Originally a platform for Nomine to release his own work, but now also home to several Dubstep/Grime and Breaks artists. Burning down walls and restrictions of the genre's limits... A 'no rules, bass orgy' - Nomine.

THE ESSENTIALS

NOMINE 'NO'

BOYLAN & SLIMZEE 'NO CURE'

ON THE EDGE

2007 - 2012

One of Z-Audio's many off-shoots, fully immersed in the melodic quarter of the scene with releases from Biome, Indigo, Synkro & V.I.V.E.K.

THE ESSENTIALS

DJ RUM 'ST. MARTIN / TENSION'

V.I.V.E.K 'NATURAL MYSTIC'

RANKING RECORDS

2007 - 2019

Early playground & foundation settings for Submotion Orchestra's Dom Ruckspin & Tommy Evans (who also formed Gentleman's Dub Club). Home to early Ruckspin, Quark, Quantum Soul & Reso Productions.

THE ESSENTIALS

QUARK 'POINT OF SEEING'

RUCKSPIN & QUANTUM SOUL 'ATOMISE'

SCRUB A DUB

2008 - 2020

Dubstep sublabel from Scotch Bonnet, run by Mungo's Hi-Fi - featuring cuts from Egoless, Somah, Traces and Von D as well as several releases by Mungo's Hi-Fi.

THE ESSENTIALS

MUNGO'S HI-FI 'RULES OF THE DANCE (KAHN REMIX)'
MUNGO'S HI-FI 'BABYLON'

SECTOR 7

2013 - PRESENT

Started in Bristol by Boofy - who's made sure the label can't be pinned down musically. With artists like Commodo, Kahn & Neek, Jook, Drone & Hi5 Ghost on the buttons, their releases don't disappoint!

THE ESSENTIALS

COMMODO 'SCABZ'

IMPEY 'BANGCLAP'

SENTRY

2017 - PRESENT

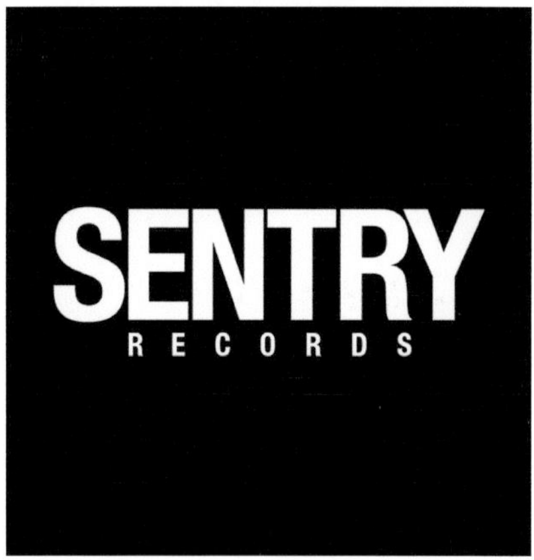

Youngsta is almost synonymous with the word Dubstep. One of the top DJs in the business, A&R at Tempa, started his own imprint with cuts from dBridge, Nomine and Akcept - and fully cemented itself into the scene!

THE ESSENTIALS

NOMINE 'STOMP'

DBRIDGE 'FASHION DREAD'

SKULL DISCO

2005 - 2008

Shortlived label from Shackleton & Appleblim, but they sure left a dent! Leaning toward Dubstep's darker, tribal and more experimental side, it mainly featured tracks by the bosses plus Peverelist!

THE ESSENTIALS

APPLEBLIM & PEVERELIST'CIRCLING'

SHACKLETON 'I AM ANIMAL'

SMOKIN SESSIONS

2007 - PRESENT

Part of the Z-Audio camp - a real mixed bag of flavours; from bassline wobblers to chilled downtempo melodic beats, plates from some of the scenes more prolific artists, such as Biome, DJ Rum, Synkro & Versa.

THE ESSENTIALS

VERSA '5AM'

S.Y.N.K.R.O 'EVERYBODY KNOWS'

SOUTHSIDE DUBSTARS

2005 - 2012

Dubstep offshoot of legendary UKG/Grime label Southside Recordings; they released tracks from dubstep royalty like N-Type, Plasticman, Kromestar, Skream & Benga. Absolutely weighty back catalogue!!

THE ESSENTIALS

KROMESTAR 'COCA COLA'
KROMESTAR 'WITCH KRAFT'

SUBALTERN

2013 - PRESENT

The roots of Dubstep are extremely important to Subaltern's owners. Releasing great soundsystem music on vinyl, putting out some amazing music from the likes of Ago, DPRTNDRP, Clearlight, Taiko & ILL_K.

THE ESSENTIALS

AGO 'BACKLASH'

ILL_K 'WARP 9'

SUB:CLEF

2017 - 2020

Sub:Clef

RECORDS

Started in 2017 by Cid Poitier as a creative output for his solo dubstep productions. Sub:Clef brings a soulful and punchy take on the genre that's a breath of fresh air.

THE ESSENTIALS

CID POTIER 'DISTRACTION (FT. WENDS)'

CID POITIER 'GRIM CREEPER'

SYSTEM

2013 - PRESENT

Started as a record label and club night V.I.V.E.K's output on both fronts has always put one thing first - the sound system. Cuts from Kromestar, Versa, SP:MC, Babe Roots, Headland, the list goes on and on. Heavy!

THE ESSENTIALS

LEWFLOW 'CLUEDUB'

DRONE 'AMPHIBIOUS'

TEMPA

2000 - 2016

Tempa.

One of the most important labels in Dubstep. Very much at the forefront of the genre's birth in the early 2000s. A&R'd by Youngsta, starting with productions from Benny Ill, Dub War & Horsepower Productions.

THE ESSENTIALS

SKREAM 'MIDNIGHT REQUEST LINE'

SP:MC 'TRUST NOBODY'

UPRISE AUDIO

2012 - 2021

Pushing the dark and stripped-back "dungeon" sound made popular in the late 2010s, Seven's record label has put out some absolute heaters in its time!

THE ESSENTIALS

SEVEN 'SHAKER'

WAYFARER 'REFLECTIONS'

WELL ROUNDED DUBS

2015 - 2022

Fair to say every Well Rounded release goes hard. Cuts so far from Chad Dubs, Foamplate, Headland, Sepia & more. Gone quiet recently, but could pop up at any time from nowhere!!

THE ESSENTIALS

HEADLAND 'LOCAL'

FOAMPLATE 'FUZZ'

WHITE PEACH

2011 - PRESENT

Blurring the lines between Dubstep and Grime over the last ten-plus years. The Bristol-based label/shop &and distributor run by Zha has housed many of the scene's new school. Certainly one to keep your eyes on...

THE ESSENTIALS

TAIKO 'JACKAL'

SIR HISS & EMZ 'ROLLING'

ZAM ZAM SOUNDS

2012 - PRESENT

Vinyl-only imprint from Portland, Oregon pushing the dubwise, soundsystem, 7" cultures. All releses come with screen printed sleeves - featuring the who's who of the modern Dubstep scene!

THE ESSENTIALS

KARMA 'CRAMPTON BEAT'

DJ MADD 'INTERSTELLAR DUB'

SOUTHSIDECIRCULARS.COM